T0199188

The Curious Mind Of Little Athena

WRITTEN BY TAMIKA JASKOLKA

ILLUSTRATIONS BY AMBADIKUMAR

WestBow Press books may be ordered through booksellers or by contacting:

WestBow Press
A Division of Thomas Nelson & Zondervan
1663 Liberty Drive
Bloomington, IN 47403
www.westbowpress.com
844-714-3454

ILLUSTRATIONS BY AMBADIKUMAR

Scripture taken from the King James Version of the Bible.

ISBN: 978-1-6642-3335-5 (sc)
ISBN: 978-1-6642-3336-2 (e)

Library of Congress Control Number: 2021909216

Print information available on the last page.

WestBow Press rev. date: 05/18/2021

WESTBOW
PRESS®
A DIVISION OF THOMAS NELSON
& ZONDERVAN

Contents

Revelation 1:8

My child I Am the great I am. I am the Alpha and Omega.

The beginning and the end for Life to come or go, my dear.

I must state when.

They are the rules no matter how gentle or cruel and the rules

I determine when they are to bend.

The longer you dwell in hell, I assure you the greater you will sin.

*But if one knocks, I will answer, just pray I let you in so do not
be a stranger to me because you are living in a life of sin.*

*Under the harshest of circumstances, I have been
known to be an incredibly good friend.*

1
Why must I go to school?

ABCDEFGHIJKLMNOPQRSTUVWXYZ

We all must go to school to learn. To learn how letters combined transcends into words. Words then transcend into sentences. Sentences finally transcend into dialect for us to communicate.

Everyone needs to learn how to speak to one another, or at least know when to stay, go, or simply when it is our turn. When and where to arrive reading directions in life so we can navigate through this world on time. Reading and speaking are the key elements of communication and communication is the key in life so you will never feel left out or behind. Let us not forget our numbers for counting and coding 1 2 3 4 5 6 7 8 9 10. Something we will learn to do adding, subtracting and multiplying time and time again.

2
Why must I grow up?

We all must grow up for it is the natural process of life. Everyone and everything must grow. As we grow, we develop, and we learn. What we learn we ultimately teach. Whether it be through our travels in life or through the job we do in life or simply through our speech. As we orbit in the universe, the Sun is the natural supplier of energy to our being, and this is what scientists teach. We develop not only intellectually but physically developing from adolescent straight into adulthood.

3
Why can't I see God?

Acts 26:13.

God being the Brightest Light we would become blind to see thee. God compounds of the greatest energy and the brightest light and purest love.

God being the purest of love in which we cannot touch nor see, however his work can be seen through the natural order of life and things on Earth and beyond in which scientists are in constant exploration of other planets or where other life could possibly be. God is everywhere we are for he loves us that much. Even when we think we are alone we are truly not alone. The presence of God is near although we may not see thee nor hear thee. God's presence is forever present in the hemisphere.

John 14:6

Although God's home is in the Heavens in which we all would like to be granted entrance into furthermore we must embrace his son Christ in order to gain entrance through the light for he is the key, the bridge, the code, and the connection to get it right. God sent his son to walk in flesh in honor of our spiritual fight.

4
Why must I play alone?

Being the only child can be lonely at times, but it can also be fun. Playing alone can teach us creativity. It can also give us a sense of our own identity. The fun part of playing alone is that you have no one to tell you if you have lost or won, limit your time with a toy or space or tell you that you are wrong to your face. No one to boss, follow or chase you around. You can push yourself to any limit building yourself up without the fear of being a letdown. Playing alone can teach us to appreciate everyone whether they are a friendly person or as quiet as a clown.

5
Why am I Black and White?

God created life and in life there are seeds to grow and God made sure we had plenty of seeds. All what we may want and all what we may need. Seeds for foods, fruits, gardens, animals, and trees. But most of all we as people are God's super seeds. We come to procreate and not discriminate. We come to love and to be loved. Mommy being a seed of African American descent and Daddy being a seed of European American descent God planted the two seeds together and created you. A beautiful combination!

6

Why does Daddy get upset when you ask him something?

Daddy suffers with PTSD: Post Traumatic Stress Disorder. Therefore, he does not handle stress very well and becomes very agitated very quickly by certain questions mommy asks him from time to time.

7

Why is Daddy on the television?

Daddy is speaking about the situation in which caused Daddy to suffer with PTSD. When Daddy was a child, he witnessed a tragedy from celebratory gun fire. Daddy's cousin was struck in the head by a bullet as they both walked down a street in South Philadelphia. Witnessing this dramatic event in which ultimately has had a profound effect on Daddy's life ever since. Daddy has gone through years of counseling as he struggles with PTSD and copes with extreme anxiety.

Matthew 26:26-52

Guns kill someone every day so never play with a gun because a life can be carelessly taken away for this sort of thing happens every single day. Having a gun requires a great deal of responsibility and unfortunately most who possess them lack the capability. In our city bullets riddle through our communities in every way killing the youth so much so we, as parents are afraid to allow our children to go out and play.

8
Why must I wait?

Galatians 6:9

We must wait for the things in which will ultimately hold a great impact in our lives. Waiting may not always make us feel good but when we wait and receive the good, we have little to no regrets. This is what one refers to as patience. Waiting builds patience and patience builds character so be still in your wait for this is something in which literally determines your fate.

9
Why must we die?

Roman's 6:23

Although one's body will perish to the earth our spirit moves on. The shear essence of who we are as individuals. This is what we refer to as one's spirit, and this is how one will go on to meet one's Creator after one is gone. Therefore, it is very necessary to always acknowledge God in all we do so He will acknowledge us when we are absent from the body and ultimately in the presence of the Almighty.

10
Why must I wear a mask when I go out?

We are all covered to protect ourselves and others from a highly contagious disease referred to as Covid-19. No one can visit anyone. You must do deep hand washing, remain at least a 6-foot distance from one another, and everyone must remain in their homes. This can be something like a dream or something like a nightmare. We all should get vaccinated to show we all are prepared to safely unveil into the open air where others may be and to be back around the ones who we absolutely love without worries or fears.

II
What Is Racism?

When a person is discriminated upon due to differences. Different skin color, texture/color of someone's hair or simply for the community they live in. Black people tend to be the focal of this sort of discrimination for all these reasons and then some, as well as, murdered due to our undying resilient nature to be treated equal as our white brothers and sisters furthermore Racism is driven by a deep-rooted hate and hate needs no specification nor justification to do harm at any time to anyone who can easily become bait. Love is the only conqueror of this decrepitated fate.

We all must stand up against the face of Hate before it is too late or we all will be held liable for the bloodshed and damage it ultimately creates. Here are some examples of the bloodshed along with the dates of Black's being murdered at an alarming rate simply through racial profiling and racism driven by hate.

Victims of fatalities through racial profiling and hate driven tactics to conflict oppression on the oppressed:

<u>In 1937 a law was passed in which it became illegal to lynch an African American in the United States of America, however it continues to be done in a modern-day formality through police brutality.</u>

1st: George Junius Stinney Jr. - June 16th, 1944 An African American child was executed for a crime he did not commit by an all-white jury. The youngest person to be executed in South Carolina.

2nd: Emmitt Till – A fourteen year old African American boy on August 28, 1955. While visiting family in Mississippi from Chicago he was brutally murdered for allegedly flirting with a white woman 4 days earlier. His murder was one of the most heinous crime in American history to be done on a child.

3rd: Carl Cooper - A seventeen-year-old, along with Aubrey Polland and Fred Temple were all shot by white Detroit police officers on July 26, 1967 while being at a party.

4th: Randolph Evans – A fifteen-year-old shot in the head at point blank range by a white New York City police officer.

5th: Arthur Miller Jr. - Was murdered by chokehold/strangulation by a white New York City police officer on June 14, 1978.

6th: Michael Jerome Stewart - On September 28, 1983 was beaten to death (Brutal force caused death) by a New York City police officer for graffiti. He was an artist making a mural.

7: Yvonne Small Wood- Born in 1959 died December 9, 1987. She was beaten by a New York City police officer in which ultimately resulted in her death.

8: Mary Mitchell- November 3, 1991 was shot by a Bronx Police Officer.

9: Frankie Ann Perkins- March 22, 1997 was murdered by Brutal force/ strangled by Chicago Police officers for running away from the officers in fear of her life.

Fast forward through the years of perpetual excessive force causing fatalities on the black citizens of America to 2020.

George Perry Floyd- May 25, 2020 in Minneapolis, a Minneapolis Police offer knelt on his neck for over 9 minutes causing Asphyxiation. Eyewitnesses recorded to whole ordeal provoking outrage and a massive protest in which resonated outside the borders of America's walls causing a nationwide out cry for justice in which ultimately ignited Black Lives Matter protests worldwide. As protests ensued as the brutality continued. Furthermore, Daunte Wright was murder by a white police officer who shot him during a traffic stop on 4/11/2021 during the 4-week trial of the murder of George Perry Floyd in the same state of Minnesota 10 miles away from the exact spot where George Perry Floyd was murdered almost a year prior. Partial justice was finally served on 4/20/2021 for George Perry Floyd. The 12-member jury convicted Dereck Chauvin the officer responsible for the death of George Floyd on all accounts in which he was being indicted on. This making history for the 1st officer to be prosecuted for the murder of a Black civilian in America. A start towards a conversation for change with police reform and judicial system within the fabric of the United States of America. As the brutality continues against black and brown people but is not limited to just brutality.

Breonna Taylor - A 26-year-old EMT worker in Louisville, Kentucky sleeping in her bed was gunned down inside her apartment in which the police were looking for someone else. The white police officers involved in the shooting remain under investigation. However, reparation in the sum of 12 million dollars was paid to her family. A small price to pay for a life stolen unjustly but this would have been swept under the proverbial shield of protection if Breanna Taylor's mother Tamika Palmer did not speak out in question of what happened to her daughter. This caught the attention of the nation once again causing a massive support from around the world, as well as relentless protests for justice for her killing.

Finally, my daughter asked me, "Mommy. Did the police kill the Black Panther?" Taken by surprise, I paused before answering thinking of all the young Black men and women robbed of their lives and could have been the next Black hero in someone else's life as the tears overflowed in my eyes my response was, "No baby. God needed a warrior in his spiritual war, so he took one of our best to help us out against bad and evil. Rest is Heavenly Peace Chadwick Boseman"

In life we must understand there is natural and supernatural, and we are compounds of both. Learn to listen to grow intellectually, be wise, be a symbol of love and be blessed.

From: *Tamika Jaskolka*

This book was written for my daughter Athena Mildred Jaskolka however this book was also created for all little girls and boys, as well as those who are seekers of the world looking for answers. I once was a seeker of the world searching for answers and birthed one as well and these are my answers to you. Be free but be wise. Education comes from an institution of educators however wisdom and unconditional love comes from God. Stay close to God and He shall stay close to you. Blessings to you and the youth for you are the future.

ME!!

Please do not look at me because I am afraid of what you may see.

Not the spirit in me but the threat from the skin in which covers me.

Although, I truly pose no threat. I must prove to everyone
that I am not a threat while being me.

Me, I am just a person who wants to be happy looking
to be free, free from harm and free from the

Disparaging remarks in which evokes preconceiving notions cast upon me.

Please help me to see you so that you may truly, see me!

About the Author

This Author gives partiticular topics of discussion with a detailed explanation in which anyone of any age group can understand. FUNDAMENTALLY, INSPIRATIONALLY AND POETICALLY.

This author was born and raised in Philadelphia,Pa.

Most of Tamika's life she longed to be a mother faced with the fear of never being able to concieve a child of her own she gave up on the notion that she would ever conceive until at the age of 42 she was Blessed by GOD himself with the greatest news on July 17, 2014. The doctor told Tamika she was pregnant in total disbelief she asked, "are you sure," before breaking down crying. Well on the 5th of February 2015 Athena Mildred Jaskolka entered into the world into her mothers arms where she continues to stay. Athena was the only baby who would not sleep in the infant incubator in the hospital she slept in her mothers arms in total content. The only time she did not have any questions for her mother and this author had no more questions for GOD for her dreams manifest themselves inside her open arms and in her life. This author has written 2 other books in which gives readers a great detail of her struggles to conceive. Titled: "The Second Time Around," AND, "The Silent Cries Of A Barbie Doll."

Printed in the United States
by Baker & Taylor Publisher Services